REMBRANDT
LIFE OF A PORTRAIT PAINTER

BY

DAVID SPENCE

THE WORLD IN THE 1650S

W hat was the world like when Rembrandt was alive? European powers were expanding their influence far and wide, with English and Dutch settlements in North America beginning to rival those of the Spanish and Portuguese in South America and the Caribbean. European trade in the East was growing with the important spice trade in the East Indies. In England there was civil war. King Charles I was executed as Oliver Cromwell's Parliamentary Army swept to power. The United Provinces of the Netherlands had finally shaken the domination of Spain by 1648, and was becoming one of the wealthiest countries in the world thanks to the strength of its seaborne empire and Dutch East India Company. In the 1650s, Russia's armies invaded the forests of China whose ruling Ming family dynasty was at an end. Japan's ruling Shogun military dictatorship expelled all foreigners from the country; Japan's borders were to be closed for over 200 years.

SHAH JAHAN & THE TAJ MAHAL

This huge and magnificent white marble building is a tomb, built in 1631 in memory of Mumtaz Mahal, wife of the Moghul emperor Shah Jahan (shown above). The building is inlaid with many precious stones and is a good example of the riches of India, which drew in the English traders in the 1600s.

RENÉ DESCARTES

The French philosopher and mathematician who lived during the first half of the 17th century is considered to have founded modern philosophy. His statement: "Cogito ergo sum" (*"I think therefore I am"*), has become famous and often quoted.

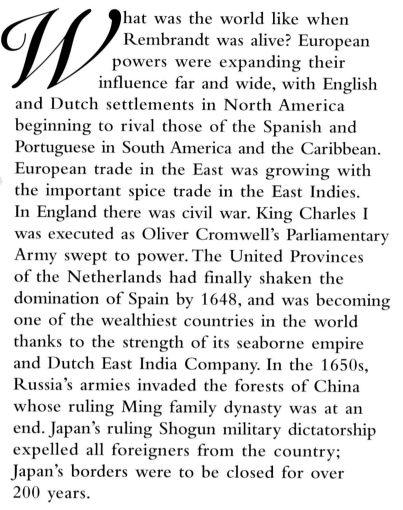

TOTIUS TERRARUM ORBIS GEOGRAPHICA AC HYDROGRAPHICA TABULA auct: Guilielmo Blaeuw

MAP OF THE WORLD, 1650

By 1650, the shape of the world was largely known. The great southern land mass of Australia was yet to be encountered, and the polar regions were still unmapped, yet the Dutch were already proficient map-makers, using the knowledge gained from their considerable merchant and navy fleets, which traveled to many parts of the globe. By 1650, New York, or New Amsterdam as it was then known, had a population of about 1500.

BLOOD CIRCULATION

The English doctor William Harvey, published an account of blood circulation in the human body. His work, from the 1620s to his death in 1657, enabled important advances in medicine. Harvey made meticulous drawings, like wiring diagrams, which demonstrated how blood circulated through the arteries and returned to the heart via the veins. His ideas were slow to gain acceptance because they contradicted the thinking of the day.

THE WORLD OF REMBRANDT

"*You can buy anything you want, you are free, and you are safe,*" said the French philosopher Descartes about Amsterdam. This was the world in which Rembrandt worked and lived, being described as "Rembrandt van Rijn, merchant, of Amsterdam" on a document dated November 1, 1642. The town was inhabited by people from many different cultures and religions: Catholics, Jews, Calvinists, and Lutherans were free to worship as they pleased. The wealthy merchants of Amsterdam were university-educated with a knowledge of languages and an appreciation of art. Rembrandt was born in Leiden, taking up residence in Amsterdam in 1633. At this time the Northern Provinces, including Holland, had become independent of Spain, although the Netherlands was not to win complete independence until 1648. Holland was prosperous and cosmopolitan, and could be said to be entering into its "golden age."

SELF-PORTRAIT, *(detail)* 1640

This portrait was painted when Rembrandt was 34 years old. By this age he had established himself as a painter, was married, and had bought a house. His marriage to Saskia van Uylenburgh was considered a good one. Rembrandt, the son of a miller, had married the daughter of a mayor; she would have brought a good dowry with her. Rembrandt purchased his own house in the Breestraat for the sum of 13,000 guilders, although he did not pay for the house immediately and was slow in making payments.

VIEW ON THE AMSTEL LOOKING TOWARDS AMSTERDAM, *Jacob Isaakszoon van Ruisdael*

Rembrandt moved to Amsterdam after his father's death in 1630. Amsterdam was the most important town in the Dutch Republic, its growth based on the shipping trade, particularly wood and grain from the Baltic ports. The foundation of the Dutch East India Company in 1602, strengthened the Dutch domination of world trade and navigation at sea, with the trade in spices and Eastern goods bringing fabulous wealth to the town. Many of the inhabitants of Amsterdam participated in "ships' share poker." By investing in shares, it was possible for all the citizens to gamble a little and make some money, or if the ship foundered, to lose their stake.

PURITAN FASHION

The clothes of the burghers of Amsterdam were plain and straightforward. As in this example, the majority of Rembrandt's portraits of well-to-do men and women, show them dressed in black clothes with white collar and cuffs. Sometimes the women wear a white cap and the more flamboyant men wear decorative lace trimmings on their shoes. Black and white was the uniform of the day, just as the suit is to us today. The fashion moved across the Atlantic to America with the Dutch settlers.

THE MILLER'S SON

Rembrandt was born in 1606, to Cornelia and Harmen Gerritsz van Rijn. His father was a prosperous malt-miller who supplied the local beer industry. Two windmills dominated the view from the family house in Leiden. The town was an important center for textiles and Leiden University was becoming well known in Europe.

A REMBRANDT TULIP

The Dutch have been famous for their tulips since the plants were first brought to Europe from the Middle East in the 16th century. Dutch flower painting often included tulips, particularly the variety which has come to be known as the Rembrandt Tulip, with its striped colors.

ENGLAND— ANTHONY VAN DYCK

Charles I of England out Hunting
A pupil of the famous Dutch artist Rubens in his home town of Antwerp, Anthony van Dyck moved to England and won the position of court painter to Charles I in 1632. Van Dyck's painting captured the refinement and elegance of the English aristocracy. Charles was a great patron of the arts, bestowing on him the title, Sir Anthony van Dyck.

FRANCE—GEORGES DE LA TOUR

Mary Magdalen
The obsession with light and shade which fills Georges de la Tour's painting is in the tradition of "baroque," which dominated much of European art. However, many famous French artists of the time, such as Poussin and Lorrain, returned to classicism.

SPAIN—DIEGO VELÁZQUEZ

Las Meninas
Court painter to the King of Spain, Velázquez portrays the world of Spanish royalty with ruthless naturalism in the tradition of the Italian artist Caravaggio, whose work impressed him so much. At the center of the painting is the Infanta Margarita Teresa, daughter of King Philip IV. The painting's title means "Maids of Honor."

ITALY—ARTEMISIA GENTILESCHI

Judith Slaying Holofernes
Artemisia Gentileschi's picture exemplifies Italian baroque. The female artist's realistic depiction is made more powerful by dramatic lighting and movement. It was unusual for women to be artists in the 17th century. They were excluded from studying the human form in life classes and as a result were more likely to execute flower paintings, than full blooded narratives like this.

THE ART OF HIS DAY

European painting became dominated by realism during the 17th century.

This was later to become known as the Baroque period. Catholic countries were influenced by Italian art, full of movement and drama, while the Northern Protestant countries such as the United Provinces of the Netherlands mirrored nature. In general, however, artists depicted people and events in a natural way, concerned with the depiction of light, form, and color as in real life. Art in the Netherlands flourished during this period more than any other. Three of the greatist artists of the 17th century came from the Netherlands. Peter Paul Rubens worked in the Catholic controlled Flemish town of Antwerp; Rembrandt in Amsterdam; Jan Vermeer in Delft near The Hague.

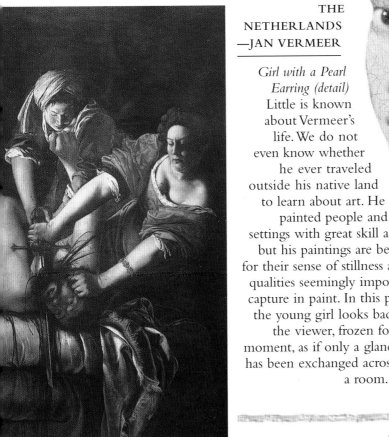

THE NETHERLANDS —JAN VERMEER

Girl with a Pearl Earring (detail) Little is known about Vermeer's life. We do not even know whether he ever traveled outside his native land to learn about art. He painted people and domestic settings with great skill and detail, but his paintings are best known for their sense of stillness and calm, qualities seemingly impossible to capture in paint. In this picture the young girl looks back at the viewer, frozen for a moment, as if only a glance has been exchanged across a room.

THE LIFE OF REMBRANDT

~1606~
Rembrandt van Rijn born in Leiden on July 15

~1621~
Becomes a pupil of the artist Jacob van Swannenburgh

~1624~
Studies with the artist Pieter Lastman in Amsterdam

~1625~
Rembrandt sets up studio in Leiden

~1630~
Rembrandt's father dies

~1632~
Rembrandt undertakes several commissions in Amsterdam and The Hague including *The Anatomy Lesson of Dr Tulp*

~1633~
Sets up home in Amsterdam lodging with Hendrick van Uylenburgh, Uncle of Saskia van Uylenburgh

~1634~
Marries Saskia and becomes a citizen of Amsterdam

~1635~
The couple move to a rented house in the Nieuwe Doelenstraat. Rombertus is born but dies two months later

~1638~
Birth of Cornelia, who dies after a month

SASKIA, 1633

Only one recorded portrait of Saskia survives. This silverpoint was made by Rembrandt on his betrothal to his wife. Rembrandt wrote underneath: *"This is drawn after my wife, when she was twenty-one years old, the third day after our betrothal—the eighth of June, 1633."* No other portrait of Saskia, or of his women friends later in life, has been identified although it is probable that they appear many times in his pictures as likenesses. Saskia's loss of her first three children was not an uncommon experience at the time. Infant mortality was very high, babies being especially vulnerable to infections, which were untreatable. Saskia's death deeply affected Rembrandt, who was working on the big commission for the civic guard (now known as *The Night Watch*) at the time. The features of the little girl in the painting (shown on page 22) appear strangely like those of his wife.

SASKIA WITH ROMBERTUS, *(detail)* 1635/36

The first child born to Saskia and Rembrandt was a boy who they named Rombertus, after Saskia's father rather than the custom of the day, which was to name the first born son after the father's father. The baby was baptized in December, 1635 but died shortly afterward.

WOMAN AT AN OPEN DOOR, 1656/57

Although no painting is officially credited as depicting Hendrickje Stoffels, she is thought to be the model for *Woman at an Open Door*. Rembrandt and Hendrickje lived as a married couple, and in 1654 they had a daughter, named Cornelia. Hendrickje was summoned to appear before the local church council who accused her of committing the acts of a prostitute and barred her from communion. Despite this the four (Rembrandt, Hendrickje, Titus, and Cornelia) lived together happily in their house in the Breestraat. Rembrandt draws attention to Hendrickje's status as common-law wife by painting a ring on her hand and a cord, on which hangs another ring, around her neck.

FAMILY & FRIENDS

Rembrandt was one of nine children, five of who died when young. His success as a painter in his late twenties was mirrored by rapid social progress when he married Saskia van Uylenburgh who brought with her a substantial dowry. Life must have seemed good to the young couple, but they were to suffer the loss of three children. The first, Rombertus, was born in 1635 but survived only two months; Cornelia, born in 1638, survived just one month; and a second daughter born in 1640, also named Cornelia, lived but a few weeks. In September 1641, a son was born and they named him Titus. He was to grow strong and survive but tragically Saskia never fully recovered from the ordeal and died just nine months later in June 1642, leaving Rembrandt a widower with a son to bring up.

TITUS, *(detail)* c1657

Rembrandt's son Titus survived into adulthood. When his mother died, Rembrandt employed a housekeeper named Geertje Dircx to help with Titus's upbringing. Rembrandt fell out with Geertje and in 1649 turned his attention to the younger Hendrickje Stoffels, who cared for Titus in the subsequent years. Titus received art lessons from his father, but he displayed no obvious inclination to follow in his father's footsteps. In 1655, Rembrandt made his house over to Titus as financial pressures mounted but was declared insolvent in 1656. By 1660, Titus and Hendrickje had set up an art dealing business, which in turn employed Rembrandt, an arrangement designed to protect him from creditors. When Titus died in 1668, a year before his father, he left a wife and a six month old daughter named Titia.

FAMILY & FAMILIAR FACES

The picture above is a detail from *Belshazzar's Feast*, c.1635 (see page 25), and bears a strong resemblance to Saskia, as shown below from the silverpoint portrait, dated 1633 (see page 8).

*R*embrandt needed inspiration for the characters in his paintings when they were not commissioned portraits. Many of the biblical and mythological scenes may have been sketched out in his mind but when it came to the detail, Rembrandt needed to paint from life. His nearest and dearest were often called on to serve as models, dressed for the part in costumes and posing in his studio. Rembrandt's first wife, Saskia, can be recognized time and again, in many different guises. Geertje Dircx, his partner after the death of Saskia, took on the role of model for a while but after they parted Hendrickje Stoffels began to appear in the paintings.

SUSANNA AND THE ELDERS, 1647

This painting portrays the story from the Apocrypha of the planned seduction of Susanna (Hebrew for Lily, meaning purity) by two elders of the community. As Susanna bathes the two men surprise her and say: *"...consent unto us and live with us. If thou wilt not, we will bear witness against thee, that a young man was with thee..."* Susanna spurned their advances so they made their false charge of adultery and Susanna was condemned to death. Daniel proved them liars and they were executed in her place. Rembrandt painted the picture in 1647, five years after Geertje Dircx had moved into his house.

The face of Geertje was used to represent Susanna, but her affair with Rembrandt ended unhappily for her. Some time around 1648, the young Hendrickje Stoffels joined the Rembrandt household and his attentions turned to her. Geertje and Rembrandt separated in anger. It is evident that she had expected to marry Rembrandt because she later sued him for breach of promise and alimony payments. Geertje pawned jewelry that had belonged to Saskia and in revenge Rembrandt arranged for her to be locked up in the workhouse for 12 years.

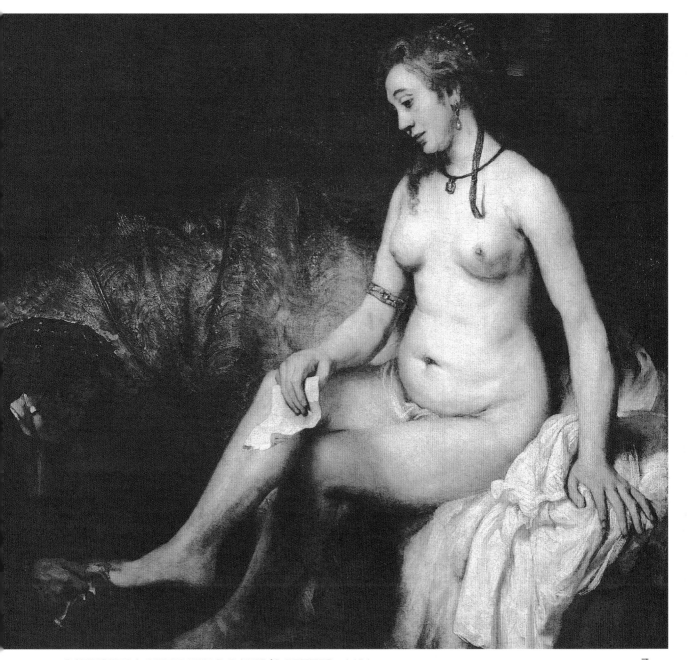

BATHSHEBA WITH KING DAVID'S LETTER, 1654

Another biblical scene, this time from the Book of Samuel, describes how King David commits adultery with Uriah's wife Bathsheba. Bathsheba becomes pregnant as a result, so David engineers Uriah's death. A story popular with artists, Rembrandt uses the scene to concentrate on the depiction of the female form.

The face of Bathsheba bears a strong resemblance to those depicted in other paintings during the 1650s, when Hendrickje Stoffels was Rembrandt's common-law wife. It may be no coincidence that this picture, telling the story of a pregnant Bathsheba, was painted in the year that Hendrickje was carrying Rembrandt's daughter.

THE LIFE OF REMBRANDT

~1640~
Birth of second daughter Cornelia who dies after three weeks. Death of Rembrandt's mother

~1641~
Birth of son Titus

~1642~
Saskia dies and is buried at the Oude Kerk. Geertje Dircx joins the household as housekeeper and nanny for Titus

11

THEATER OF ANATOMY AT LEIDEN

The study of anatomy was advanced by the dissection of corpses. It was permissible to dissect the corpses of executed criminals, but this was possible only a few times a year. When a dissection did take place large crowds of students and sightseers gathered, paying for the privilege of watching the spectacle.

IN & ABOUT TOWN

No records of any diaries kept by Rembrandt exist today and only a few letters survive, but the chronology of his life is well understood thanks to a great deal of painstaking research by many Rembrandt scholars. Rembrandt's family were millers and he grew up in Leiden with his parents, brothers, and younger sister in a small house facing the river next to the family windmill. He went to university at 14, but decided that he wanted to pursue a career as a painter and was apprenticed to the studio of Jacob van Swannenburgh. The apprentice had to master drawing, the art of mixing colors, the theory of perspective, and how to imitate the style of his master—even to better it —but not to be original.

Having done this Rembrandt could become a member of an artist's guild and sell paintings in his own right. He moved to Amsterdam and despite the fact that he did not appear to establish himself with the artist's guild, his work became very much in demand. Rembrandt van Rijn, artist, made a good marriage to Saskia van Uylenburgh whose inheritance should have set them up for life.

HAPPY FAMILIES

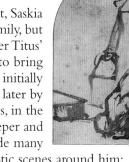

For a time Rembrandt, Saskia and, Titus were a family, but Saskia died not long after Titus' birth. Rembrandt had to bring up the little boy, aided initially by Geertje Dircx and later by Hendrickje Stoffels, in the roles of nurse, housekeeper and "partner." He made many sketches of the domestic scenes around him; young children as they were coaxed to eat; as they had their tantrums; as they learned to walk.

THE ZUIDERKERK

The infant mortality rate across Europe in the 17th century was well over 50 percent. The first three babies born to Saskia and Rembrandt died when they were very young. They were buried in the local church, the Zuiderkerk, which eventually had a happier significance for them as their fourth child, Titus, was baptized there in September, 1641.

REMBRANDT'S HOUSE

Rembrandt and Saskia moved into Number 4, Breestraat on May 1, 1639. They were to live there for the next 20 years. Records show that Rembrandt was slow to pay for the house even by the standards of the day. When he was made insolvent in 1656, the house had to be sold to pay his creditors.

RETURN OF THE DUTCH EAST INDIA FLEET

Amsterdam was the center for north European sea-trade and the city's wealth was generated by commerce with the East. Descartes, who lived in Amsterdam, wrote in 1631: *"If there is pleasure in seeing the fruits of our orchard grow, don't you think there will be as much in seeing ships arriving bringing us in abundance all that the Indies produce and all that is rare in Europe? What other country could one choose where all the conveniences of life and all the exotic things one could desire are found so easily?"*

The contemporary view quite clearly illustrated in this passage is that the world was a fruitful "orchard" to be cultivated by the Dutch in order that they could harvest its wealth for their benefit. Rembrandt owned a pair 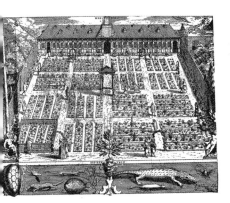 of globes and could trace the voyages of the ships that were to benefit the merchants of Amsterdam and so benefit him.

RESTING PLACE

Hendrickje died on July 24, 1663, and had a simple burial in the local church, the Westerkerk. Titus died in 1668 and again was buried in the Westerkerk. On October 4, 1669, aged 63 years, Rembrandt died and was buried alongside his son and partner. We do not know what he died of, and his grave in the cemetery at the Westerkerk has never been identified.

THE BOTANICAL GARDENS AT LEIDEN UNIVERSITY

Leiden University, founded in 1575, had an excellent reputation throughout Europe for its medical, scientific, and theological studies. The university was well known for its botanical garden which cultivated plants thought to be of medicinal value.

WHAT DO THE PAINTINGS SAY?

Rembrandt's commissioned portrait work took him from his home town of Leiden to Amsterdam, where he eventually settled. In 1632, Rembrandt painted one of the most important commissions in his career, that of *The Anatomy Lesson of Dr Nicolaes Tulp*. The dissection of corpses was considered illegal until shortly before Rembrandt's time, and then it was only the corpses of criminals which could be dissected. Dissections took place in lecture halls for teaching purposes. These halls were based on circular theaters with banked seats, and were called Theaters of Anatomy. In 1632 it was not uncommon for the professors and medical students to be joined by the public at large, seated on the outer benches, drawn by the macabre novelty of the occasion.

Calcoen holds in his left hand the top of the skull of Joris Fonteijn, hanged for robbery the previous day. His right hand is turned back away from his body to prevent blood from the corpse getting on his clothes.

THE ANATOMY LESSON OF DR JOAN DEYMAN, 1656

This picture was painted in 1656, some 24 years after the first anatomy picture, and it is a credit to Rembrandt's standing that the Guild of Surgeons returned to him for this commission. This too was a group portrait but much of the painting was destroyed by fire in 1723, leaving us today with only the central section. Dr Deyman's hands can be seen performing a dissection of the brain. Deyman, Tulp's successor as Praelector (lecturer), was originally surrounded by the guild members, but only Gysbrecht Matthijsz Calcoen, Master of the Amsterdam Guild of Surgeons, survives.

Deyman performed three anatomical demonstrations, for which he was presented with six silver spoons and an amount in cash (19 stuivers), as well as income from the sale of tickets to the demonstrations, before the corpse was buried on February 2.

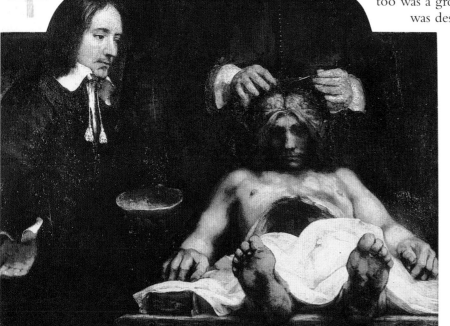

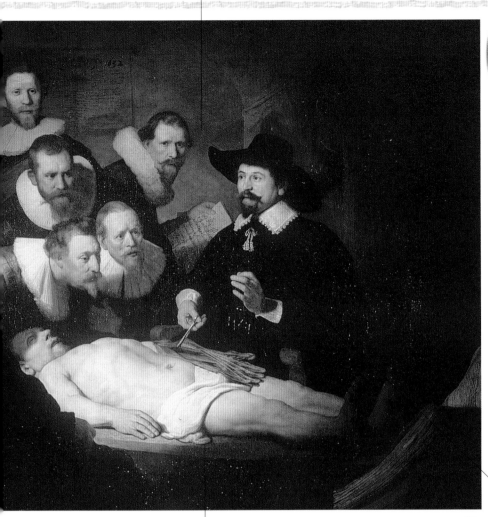

The corpse is that of Adriaen Adriaansz, known as "the Kid," who was executed for robbery. The identity of Tulp's colleagues is known because they are written on the paper held by the figure depicted behind Tulp. Number 6 on the paper is Matthijsz Calcoen, whose son Gysbrecht is portrayed in Rembrandt's picture of *The Anatomy Lesson of Dr Deyman*. At the corpse's feet is propped open a book of anatomy.

THE ANATOMY LESSON OF DR NICOLAES TULP, 1632

This painting for the Amsterdam Guild of Surgeons, was the first important public commission Rembrandt received in Amsterdam. It shows lecturer in anatomy Dr Nicolaes Tulp, surrounded by his colleagues. He wears a broad brimmed hat which signified his high status in the Guild. Tulp lectured twice a week in the Anatomy Theater in the upper story of the meat market building, although actual dissections were infrequent, perhaps two or three a year.

Tulp is dissecting the tendons that flex the hand. With his left hand he demonstrates the flexing action made possible by the tendons. It may be that Rembrandt wanted to make a particular point about the importance of the hand to surgeon and artist alike, because normal practice would have dealt with body first and extremities last, mainly because of the bad odor.

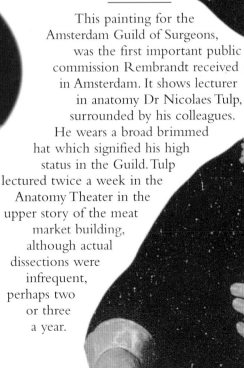

THE RICH MAN FROM THE PARABLE, 1627

This has been identified as the Parable of the Rich Fool from the Book of Luke (12:13). An old man studies a coin by the light of a candle; surrounding him are tally sheets and ledgers with Hebrew script and bags of money. The story from the Bible tells of a man who becomes rich after fruitful harvests. He pulls down his barns to build bigger ones and lives off the stored riches. But: *"…God said, 'Thou fool, this night thy soul shall be required of thee, then whose shall those things be, which thou hast provided? So is he that layeth up treasure for himself, and is not rich towards God.'"*

Rembrandt paints the scene on the very night that the rich man's soul shall be required. In the shadows stands a clock, symbolizing that his time is about to run out.

In front of him on the table are the goldsmith's scales.

WHAT DO THE PAINTINGS SAY?

The Bible was the source of inspiration for a large number of Rembrandt's paintings. Rembrandt turned especially to the Old Testament stories, which he painted as convincing scenes from history. He may have been influenced in his subject matter by his many Jewish friends and neighbors. Rembrandt lived in an area of Leiden populated by Jews and we know he often spent time in deep discussion with these friends. These pictures were largely imaginary scenes, but populated with models or figurative references to existing paintings. Painting these pictures enabled Rembrandt to create the scenes he must have imagined in his head when as a boy, his mother read these Old and New Testament stories to him.

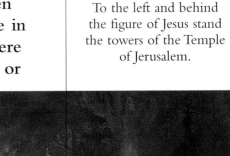

To the left and behind the figure of Jesus stand the towers of the Temple of Jerusalem.

JESUS AS A GARDENER

Rembrandt paints the moment when Mary realizes that the man standing behind her is not the gardener but in fact Jesus, risen from the dead. Rembrandt makes the story recognizable by placing a gardener's hat on Jesus' head and a spade in his hand.

CHRIST AND ST. MARY MAGDALEN AT THE TOMB, 1638

This painting, which tells the story of Mary Magdalen's encounter with Jesus after the resurrection, is typical of Rembrandt's history painting. The depiction of classical history, mythology, or biblical stories was a strong tradition in art and considered for many years to be the highest form of art. The term "history painting" does in fact mean to tell a story (the French word for story is *histoire*), and we should remember that the artist is telling a story about an historical event. In this painting, Mary Magdalen has returned to the empty tomb and on seeing two angels who ask her why she is crying, Mary answers: *"Because they have taken away my Lord, and I know not where they have laid him."* Rembrandt's scene attempts to capture the moment of truth for Mary Magdalen, emphasized by the light which falls on her surprised face, rather than the point in the story usually depicted by artists when Mary reaches to touch Jesus to confirm what her eyes have seen. Jesus then replies *"Touch me not"* (noli me tangere).

Rembrandt includes the jar of ointment and the cloth with which Mary Magdalen intended to anoint the body of Jesus.

SELF-PORTRAIT, c1661

Perhaps one of the best known of all Rembrandt's self-portraits, this was painted in about 1661, when he was 55. In this painting Rembrandt shows us the working artist, with palette, brushes, and maulstick in hand. This is a man who is stripped of all pretension and stands resolute despite the problems that have befallen him. He was by now a widower, having suffered the loss of three children shortly after birth as well as his wife, and was bankrupt. His partner and surviving son, Titus, saved him from ruin by forming a firm of art dealers and employing Rembrandt, enabling him to continue painting.

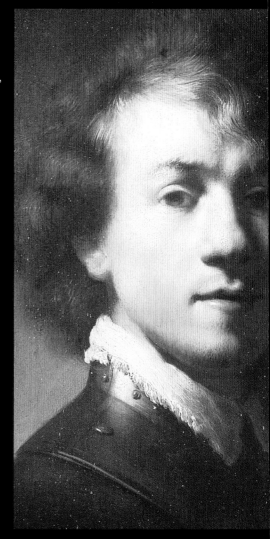

SELF-PORTRAIT AS A YOUNG MAN, 1629

At the age of 23, Rembrandt portrays a proud and elegant young man. He has given himself a fashionable lovelock across his forehead and made his nose less bulbous than it probably was in reality, by careful use of light and shadow. He had studied painting in Leiden from the age of 15, and set up as an artist sharing a studio with Jan Lievens from about 1625. By 1629, Rembrandt had begun to find a market for his pictures nearby in The Hague.

SELF-PORTRAIT, c1640

A more mature Rembrandt looks out at us in this picture despite his relative youth at only 34. The painting is clearly based upon a picture by the 16th-century Italian master Titian, called *Portrait of a Young Man* (now in the National Gallery, London). It is likely that Rembrandt had come across the Titian painting while it was in the possession of the merchant Alfonso Lopez who lived in Amsterdam at the time. Interestingly Rembrandt has dressed himself not in contemporary clothes but in the earlier style of the 16th century, and may have been imitating the fashion of the Italian man in Titian's portrait.

WHAT DO THE PAINTINGS SAY?

Rembrandt left us a series of self-portraits which covered all of his life as an artist. It is by this extraordinary record that we have come to know him through the stages of his life; the successful young painter; the lonely widower; the bankrupt; the old man. What comes across in all these pictures is a directness, an honesty not only to examine the true physical appearance but a lack of vanity. This is the Rembrandt who created the great portraits of men and women around him, which tell us about Dutch life in the 1600s. Rembrandt's self-examination has created a precedent which many artists have followed.

SELF-PORTRAIT,
(detail) c1669

Probably the last self-portrait and certainly made in his last year of life, Rembrandt now looks every bit of his 63 years. He is now alone apart from his grand-daughter Titia. His partner Hendrickje Stoffels is dead as is his son, Titus, who died a year earlier in February, 1668. When Rembrandt died on October 4, 1669, he left nothing but some clothes and his paints.

HOW WERE THEY MADE?

*P*ainting in the age of Rembrandt was a highly skilled profession that required a good technical understanding of how to make and use paint, as well as how to create an illusion on a flat plane. A great deal of investigation has gone into the methods used by Rembrandt. Paintings have been ascribed to Rembrandt and others have been judged not to be by Rembrandt as a result of these investigations. It is impossible to know with certainty whether the paintings we say today are by the master's hand include all of his works, or for that matter do not include some by other artists, perhaps studio apprentices of Rembrandt. It was common practice for studio assistants to help with the painting of large canvases, the master painting the important features, but there is no evidence that Rembrandt's studio pupils did so. Some pupils did however copy Rembrandt's style closely and it is easy to see how they might be mistaken for Rembrandt's own hand after a period of several hundred years.

BENEATH THE SURFACE

Some paintings were made on oak panels, some on canvas. The surface was prepared with a white ground base. This was either a chalk mix in the case of wooden panels, or white oil paint in the case of canvas. It is likely that Rembrandt used a paint called *Hollands lootwit* to prepare the surface, a mixture of lead white and chalk (above) that was commonly available in Amsterdam. It was normal practice to tint the ground with a brown layer of paint which was then covered with further layers of transparent color. The underpainting was known as "dead color." The artist built up a complete monochrome picture filling in all the compositional features, including the light and dark tones.

CREATING COLORS

Making colors could be a laborious process. A color often used by Rembrandt was lead-tin yellow. In order to obtain this it was necessary to melt lead in a stone crucible, add tin at high temperature, and remove the lead-tin yellow which had formed on the surface of the molten metal.

THE ARTIST IN HIS STUDIO, 1628

This is thought to be a self-portrait of the artist in his studio in Leiden in about 1629. Rembrandt holds a palette, maulstick, and brushes in his hand. Behind him stands a grinding-stone on which pigments would have been ground for mixing with the oil medium prior to painting. Two clean palettes hang on the wall, ready for use.

THE COLOR SOURCE

Rembrandt had color pigments ground into powder before mixing them with oil and then applying the colors over the underpainting. Both charred oak (left) and charred deer antler (for bone black), were ground as a source of black pigment. Willow or vine was charred to make charcoal sticks for drawing. When the colors were ready they were applied area by area rather than across the whole picture in one go, as artists have tended to do since the 19th century. Rembrandt's paintings are famous for the experimental ways in which he applied paint, a mixture of smooth glazes (transparent layers), and impasto (thick rough textured paint), which can make some pictures look very modern.

21

Toward the back stands Jan Visscher Cornelisz, the ensign holding aloft the coat-of-arms of Amsterdam with its bands of blue and gold, with embroidered lions.

At the back stands the troop jester in top hat, tentatively identified as Amsterdam wine merchant, Walich Schellingwou.

It would seem that the members of the guard paid about 100 guilders each for the commission, some more, some less depending on the place they had in it.

Perhaps the most mysterious figures are the two young girls who run between the soldiers, one almost completely obscured by the other. The foremost is dressed in bright yellow, and has a chicken tied by its legs to her belt. One supposition is that she is a carrier to a banquet, another is that the guard is turning out for target practice and the chicken is one of the targets.

The "powder monkey" with his powder horn hanging around his neck runs blind, sight obscured by the oversize helmet.

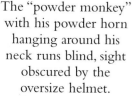

Rembrandt shows the three stages of musketry; the figure on the left in red loads the musket; the figure immediately behind Banning Cocq fires; the figure behind Ruytenburch blows away the used powder from the musket pan.

FAMOUS IMAGES

The most famous of all Rembrandt's paintings is *The Night Watch*. This group portrait painted in 1642, is of the local Amsterdam civil guard led by Captain Frans Banning Cocq and Lieutenant Willem van Ruytenburch. There was a strong tradition of these militia paintings in Amsterdam by the time Rembrandt made this one. The title is now familiar all over the world but it is misleading. It comes from the belief that the militia are being turned out at night because of the dark nature of the picture, but this was in fact due to the darkening varnish and accumulation of dirt over the years. Restoration and cleaning in the 20th century revealed the painting to show a daytime scene. The original title of the painting, as so often in the case of Rembrandt, is unknown to us. The painting was commissioned as a portrait of the civic guard who were among the more important citizens of Amsterdam. The painting was to be displayed in the Great Hall of the Civic Guards, the Kloveniersdoelen. Rembrandt had lived next door to this hall for a time. What sets Rembrandt's picture apart from the traditional style is the sense of movement and action. In the more formal group portrait, reality is sacrificed for the sake of equal emphasis on all portrayed.

At the center of the painting stands Captain Frans Banning Cocq, dressed in the black of the governing class. He was not only captain of the civic guard, but also Lord of the Manor of Purmerland, and Ilpendam councilor, and future colonel.

Beside Cocq stands Lieutenant Willem van Ruytenburch resplendent in yellow with white and gold, and boots and spurs. He was also the Lord of the Manor of Vlaerdingen.

FAMOUS IMAGES

*I*t is hard to say whether Rembrandt was a religious person. There are no records to indicate that he belonged to a particular church or sect, but we do know that the religious tolerance demonstrated in Amsterdam at the time means he would have mixed with people of different beliefs. The Jewish community in Amsterdam was largely a result of Jews escaping from religious persecution in Spain and Portugal. Rembrandt had many Jewish friends and acquaintances, and perhaps it was their influence that led him to paint Old Testament themes such as Belshazzar's Feast, based on Daniel Chapter 5:

"In the same hour came forth fingers of a man's hand, and wrote over against the candlestick upon the plaister of the wall of the king's palace; and the king saw the part of the hand that wrote.

"Then the king's countenance changed, and his thoughts troubled him, so that the joints of his loins were loosed, and his knees smote one against another."

King Belshazzar is struck with terror. His light profile against the dark background draws the viewer's eye to his face and the drama of the moment. His head-dress (turban and crown) is largely imagined because Rembrandt had no actual reference for the figures.

The woman behind Belshazzar registers open-mouthed surprise as the hand appears. The face is very like that of Saskia, Rembrandt's first wife, who probably posed for the scene.

PORTRAIT OF MENASSEH BEN ISRAEL

Menasseh was a Rabbi who lived across the street from Rembrandt. His family had fled the religious inquisitions in their home country of Portugal. Menasseh was a learned man who taught and published books, as well as preaching in the local synagogue. He and Rembrandt became good friends who often passed time discussing religious subjects, such as the problem of how the hand in the story of Belshazzar could have written a message which could only be deciphered by Daniel. Menasseh published a book in 1639, which explained how the letters could be written to give hidden messages by using a secret code. Rembrandt adopted this for his painting.

Rembrandt went to great lengths to ensure that the Hebrew words were authentic. The message reads: "Mene mene tekel upharsin," which translates as: "God hath numbered thy kingdom, and brought it to an end. Thou art weighed in the balances and art found wanting. Thy kingdom is divided, and given to the Medes and Persians." The letters read vertically rather than horizontally, and from right to left. This would explain why in the Old Testament story Belshazzar's men could not understand the message but Daniel, who knew the secret way of writing the Jewish letters, could read it.

BELSHAZZAR'S FEAST, 1635

The story tells of how Belshazzar, King of Babylon, laid on a feast for his wives, concubines, and friends, and praised the: *"...gods of gold and of silver, and of brass, of iron, of wood, and of stone."* He served the wine in vessels which his father, Nebuchadnezzar, had looted from the Temple in Jerusalem. During the feast a mysterious hand appeared and wrote a message on the wall. Belshazzar offered a reward including a gold chain to whoever could decipher the message. Only the prophet Daniel could read the writing which foretold the loss of Belshazzar's kingdom and his imminent death. That night the city was overrun, Belshazzar was killed, and the kingdom taken by Darius of the Medes.

Rembrandt's depiction of the woman on the right attempts ambitious foreshortening. The scene is reminiscent of the Italian baroque style with dramatic movement and light. Note the wine soaking into the sleeve of the woman's dress.

REMBRANDT'S PATRONS

There was a ready market for paintings in Holland in the 17th century. Artists would paint scenes and citizens of all classes would buy these paintings. Some artists however specialized in commissioned works, and prices for pictures would be calculated on the hours spent by the artist working on them. There is for example a record of the artist Adriaen van der Werff (1659–1722) charging 45 guilders per day. A painting would typically take 10 weeks to complete—thus the cost would be 3,150 guilders. It was necessary for artists who relied on commissions to entertain their patrons and socialize in the right circles. It appeared that Rembrandt would have none of this.

He did not show any interest in winning influential friends and even alienated customers whose portraits he painted by insisting they sit for unacceptably long hours. Rembrandt sometimes delayed finishing paintings, and on several occasions the paintings were returned by customers unhappy that they were not finished to their satisfaction.

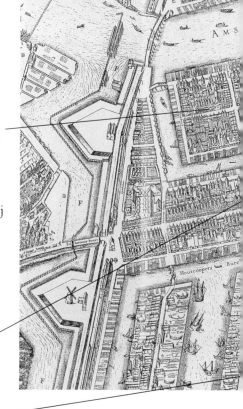

The Suyckerbackerij on Binnen-Amstel, Rembrandt's home from 1637–1639.

Number 2-4 Jodenbreestraat, Rembrandt's home from 1639-1658. Rembrandt was forced to sell his home in the Breestraat and moved to Number 184 Rozengracht where he lived until his death in 1669.

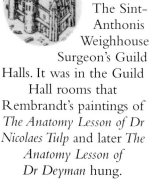

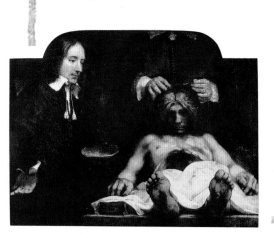

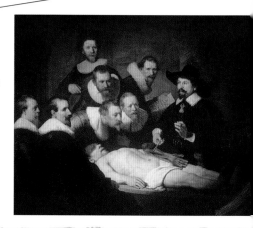

The Sint-Anthonis Weighhouse Surgeon's Guild Halls. It was in the Guild Hall rooms that Rembrandt's paintings of *The Anatomy Lesson of Dr Nicolaes Tulp* and later *The Anatomy Lesson of Dr Deyman* hung.

The Kloveniersdoelen, where *The Night Watch* hung in the Grand Hall. Rembrandt lived next door at number 20 Nieuwe Doelenstraat between 1635 and 1637, and must have seen the civic guard turn out many times.

PORTRAIT OF JAN SIX (*detail*)

At number 103 Kloveniersburgwal lived burgomaster Jan Six. Six was a friend and patron of Rembrandt, buying at least three paintings, and in 1653 loaning Rembrandt 1,000 guilders. In 1654, Rembrandt painted a magnificent portrait of Six which can still be seen in Amsterdam today.

REMBRANDT'S AMSTERDAM

Van Berkenrode's map of Amsterdam shows the district where Rembrandt lived. The destination for many of his pictures could be found within a short walk of his house. Many of his commissions were for wealthy local merchants, others for civic patrons such as the civic guard and surgeon's guild. Within a short walk of Rembrandt's house stood the local Synagogue where his good friend Menasseh ben Israel preached. This map illustrates just a few of the many local places where Rembrandt's paintings hung.

SALOME WITH THE HEAD OF JOHN THE BAPTIST

Titian

The work of Titian was widely admired throughout Europe by the time of Rembrandt, even though he had died only 30 years before Rembrandt's birth. Italian writer Giorgio Vasari described Titian's work in a book about his life which was translated into Dutch in 1604. Vasari describes Titian's technique for his later paintings as "pittura di macchia" (painting with splotches). At the time this was put down to Titian's old age and failing eyesight but today we understand it to be a deliberately freer style, painting directly without preparing the canvas with drawings. This freer style has had a huge impact on the way painting has developed.

DETAIL FROM THE PORTRAIT OF JAN SIX

Critics have pointed out that Rembrandt would have been aware of the "rough" splotchy style of Titian as opposed to the dominant "smooth" style in Holland at the time. It is quite clear from this detail of the *Portrait of Jan Six* (see page 27), painted in 1654, that Rembrandt adopted the direct method of painting with brush strokes rapidly and freely, applied to describe form and color. For the picture to be fully appreciated it should be viewed from a certain distance, as Rembrandt himself pointed out when referring to another painting in a letter to a friend. Confirmation of this may be found in a story by writer Arnold Houbraken in 1718, relating that Rembrandt would prevent viewers in his studio getting too close to his canvases, allegedly because they would be bothered by the smell of paint.

WHAT THE CRITICS SAY

Critics have been assessing the works of Rembrandt for the last 300 years and as with all artists, his work has been in and out of favor with the passing of time. Today, however, all acknowledge him as one of the greatest painters in the history of art. It has sometimes been difficult for historians to recognize Rembrandt's paintings among the many works which are said to be by the master's hand. The difference between a painting acknowledged to be by Rembrandt and that of an apprentice is great if measured in financial terms. But if a painting thought to be by Rembrandt, such as the *Man with the Golden Helmet*, is then pronounced by the art historians to be by an apprentice, how does it change in our eyes? Is it a lesser picture because we know it is not a Rembrandt, is our enjoyment of it less?

PORTRAIT OF A WOMAN *(detail) Govert Flinck*

Flinck was a pupil of Rembrandt, working in his studio and painting in the style of the master. One of the reasons why it has become difficult to judge what is a "genuine" Rembrandt and what is not after so many intervening years, is that many paintings by pupils and others were painted in the exact style of Rembrandt. At the beginning of the 20th century critics acknowledged the existence of about 1,000 paintings by Rembrandt. As successive scholars have continued to look at his paintings and applied scientific methods of dating and examination this number has gradually fallen. Doubtless as the work continues the number of "real" Rembrandt paintings may fall still further.

THE JEWISH BRIDE

Another great artist, Vincent van Gogh, visited the Rijksmuseum in Amsterdam in 1885 and said this about Rembrandt's painting of *The Jewish Bride*: *"Do you know that I would give ten years of my life if I could sit here before this picture a fortnight, with nothing but a crust of dry bread for food."*

STUDY FOR THE SURPRISED NYMPH, 1859–1861

Edouard Manet

This painting by Manet was inspired by Rembrandt's *Susanna and the Elders* (shown below), and *Bathsheba with King David's Letter* painted over 200 years earlier. The subject is timeless, the interpretation different each time. Manet's model is that of his wife Suzanne Leenhoff.

THE REMBRANDT ROOM AT THE NATIONAL GALLERY, LONDON

Each year literally millions of visitors pass through the museums and galleries that contain works by Rembrandt. The National Gallery in London is a typical example, having a fine collection of Rembrandt pictures on show, but how many people really look at the paintings? Despite all the words in all the books written about Rembrandt and his art, there is only one way to truly appreciate the artist: go and look at his paintings.

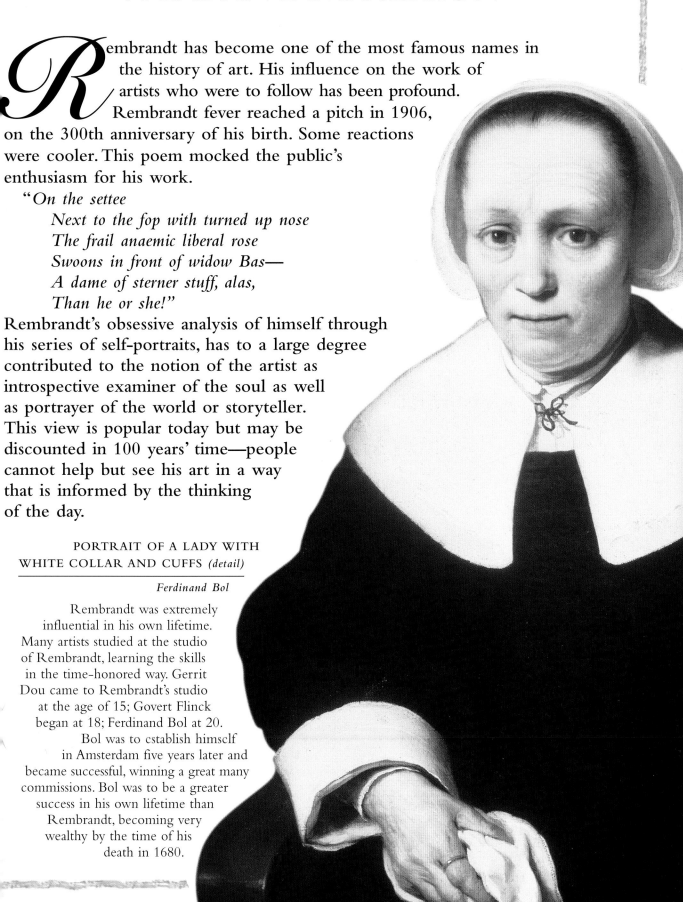

A LASTING IMPRESSION

Rembrandt has become one of the most famous names in the history of art. His influence on the work of artists who were to follow has been profound. Rembrandt fever reached a pitch in 1906, on the 300th anniversary of his birth. Some reactions were cooler. This poem mocked the public's enthusiasm for his work.

"*On the settee*
   Next to the fop with turned up nose
   The frail anaemic liberal rose
   Swoons in front of widow Bas—
   A dame of sterner stuff, alas,
   Than he or she!"

Rembrandt's obsessive analysis of himself through his series of self-portraits, has to a large degree contributed to the notion of the artist as introspective examiner of the soul as well as portrayer of the world or storyteller. This view is popular today but may be discounted in 100 years' time—people cannot help but see his art in a way that is informed by the thinking of the day.

PORTRAIT OF A LADY WITH
WHITE COLLAR AND CUFFS *(detail)*

Ferdinand Bol

Rembrandt was extremely influential in his own lifetime. Many artists studied at the studio of Rembrandt, learning the skills in the time-honored way. Gerrit Dou came to Rembrandt's studio at the age of 15; Govert Flinck began at 18; Ferdinand Bol at 20. Bol was to establish himself in Amsterdam five years later and became successful, winning a great many commissions. Bol was to be a greater success in his own lifetime than Rembrandt, becoming very wealthy by the time of his death in 1680.

GLOSSARY

Burgher—The name given to respectable citizens of the trading class. The description was most commonly used in Holland and Germany.

Flora—Rembrandt chose to paint Saskia as Flora, the Italian goddess of flowers and spring. The myth tells of a nymph named Chloris being changed into Flora by Zephyr (the warm west wind) resulting in flowers coming from Flora's breath.

Judith and Holofernes—The story of Judith and Holofernes is a favorite subject for artists. Judith was the widow from the Jewish city of Bethulia, which was under siege from the Assyrian army. She tricked her way into the confidence of Holofernes, the Assryian General, then cut off his head, so causing the army to flee and saving the city.

Maulstick—A long wooden stick with a wrapping of leather or cloth over the end to make a soft pad. The padded end rests against the canvas to provide a support for the artist's hand as he paints fine details.

Noli me tangere—This translates as "touch me not" and refers to the biblical scene which describes the moment after the Resurrection of Christ when Mary Magdalene recognizes Christ and stretches out her hand to touch him. Christ says "touch me not" and tells her to go to the disciples and tell them he is risen.

Silverpoint—A method of drawing where a piece of silver wire held in wood, like a pencil, is used to draw on paper coated with opaque white. The mark left by the silver wire will not smudge and is indelible.

ACKNOWLEDGEMENTS

North American edition Copyright © 2010 *ticktock* Entertainment Ltd.,
First published in North America by *ticktock* Media Ltd.,
The Old Sawmill, 103 Goods Station Road, Tunbridge Wells, Kent, TN1 2DP, UK.
All rights reserved. No part of this publication may be reproduced, copied, stored in a retrieval system or transmitted in any form or by any means electronic, mechanical, photocopying, recording or otherwise without prior written permission of the copyright owner.

ISBN 978 1 84696 977 5
tracking number; 3223LPP1109
Printed in China.
9 8 7 6 5 4 3 2 1

Picture Credits t=top, b=bottom, c=center, l=left, r=right, OFC=outside front cover,
IFC=inside front cover, IBC=inside back cover, OBC=outside back cover.

Akademie der Bildenden Kuenste, Vienna. Photo © AKG London/Erich Lessing; 5cl. Photo © AKG London; 3t, 6/7ct. Photo credit: Bridgeman Art Library, London; 2bl. By permission of The British Library (1790b 21 Sheet 3); 26/27c. Copyright © British Museum; 12/13c. Christie's Images/Bridgeman Art Library, London; 28tr. Courtauld Gallery, London/Bridgeman Art Library, London; 8c. Dahlem Staatliche Gemaldegalerie, Berlin/Bridgeman Art Library, London; 10bl & 30cr. Fitzwilliam Museum, University of Cambridge/Bridgeman Art Library, London; 5t. Galleria degli Uffizi, Florence. Photo © AKG London; 7bl. Kenwood House, London/Bridgeman Art Library, London; 18tl. Mary Evans Picture Library; 3bl, 3br. Mauritshuis, The Hague. Photo © AKG London; 7br. Mauritshuis, The Hague. Photo © AKG London/Erich Lessing; 15tl & 26br. Mauritshuis, The Hague/Bridgeman Art Library, London; OBC & 18cr, OFCl & 19br. Musee du Louvre, Paris. Photo © AKG London; 6tl. Musee du Louvre, Paris. Photo © AKG London/Erich Lessing; 6cr, 11t. Museo del Prado, Madrid. Photo © AKG London/Erich Lessing; 6cl. Nasjonalgalleriet, Oslo/Giraudon/Bridgeman Art Library, London; 30cl. Reproduced by courtesy of the Trustees, The National Gallery, London; 4bl & 18bl, 30br. National Gallery, London/Bridgeman Art Library, London; OFCr & 25. National Maritime Museum, London; 13tl. Private Collection, Amsterdam/Bridgeman Art Library, London; 27br. Rafael Valls Gallery, London/Bridgeman Art Library, London; 31r. Rijksmuseum, Amsterdam. Photo © AKG London; OBC & IFC/1 & 22/23 & 27tr, 14bl & 26bl, 30tr. The Royal Collection © Her Majesty Queen Elizabeth II; 17. © Sidney Moulds/Garden Picture Library; 4br. SMPK, Gemaeldegalerie, Berlin. Photo © AKG London; 8br, OBC & 16t. Staatliches Kunstmuseum, Bucharest. Photo © AKG London; 29r. Victoria & Albert Museum, London/Bridgeman Art Library, London; 2tl. Wallace Collection, London/Bridgeman Art Library, London; 9br. Zoë Oliver Sherman Collection. Given in memory of Lillie Oliver Poor. Courtesy of Museum of Fine Arts, Boston; 21t.

Every effort has been made to trace the copyright holders and we apologize in advance for any unintentional omissions.
We would be pleased to insert the appropriate acknowledgement in any subsequent edition of this publication.